ARF AND THE THREE DOGS

Philip Wooderson

Illustrated by Bridget MacKeith

A & C Black • London

comix

Published 2002 by A & C Black Publishers Ltd
37 Soho Square, London W1D 3QZ
www.acblack.com

Text copyright © 2002 Philip Wooderson
Illustrations copyright © 2002 Bridget MacKeith

The rights of Philip Wooderson and Bridget MacKeith to be identified
as author and illustrator of this work have been asserted by them in
accordance with the Copyrights, Designs and Patents Act 1988.

ISBN 0-7136-6273-5

A & C Black uses paper produced with elemental, chlorine-free pulp,
harvested from managed sustainable forests.

Printed and bound in Spain by G. Z. Printek, Bilbao

CHAPTER ONE

It was Saturday morning.

I'm bored.

Right, Arf. Take Hoppa down to the shop and pick up my local paper.

Okay. How much will you pay me?

'Mum doesn't have to pay you, Arf. You didn't pay her for your breakfast,' said Gloria. She was Arf's older sister.

She's not trying to save up like I am.

As Arf went into the shop he was practically knocked off his feet by two big dogs, on leads, dragging along an old man...

...and a little dog being dragged behind.

Oi, look where you're going!

The shop assistant helped Arf to rebuild the stack of baked beans.

Arf picked up a tattered envelope and turned it over.

Arf hurried out of the shop. He looked left and right. Left again. But there was no sign of Barney.

CHAPTER TWO

When Arf got home at last, he found Mum waiting. She sighed.

Where's my newspaper, Arf?

Oh drat it, I forgot that.

But that's all I sent you out for. What were you thinking about?

I was thinking about earning money. I might get a Saturday job.

You total idiot, Arf. What sort of job could you do?

Mr Sanjay lived at Number 3. He worked for the local paper.

You'll have to wait a long time, Arf, for something to happen around here.

But then, as if by magic, Arf looked out of the window and saw the old man with his two big dogs and...

WOOF.

But Arf walked up and down the streets for more than half an hour without finding Barmy Barney.

He was just about ready to give up when he stopped outside the pet sanctuary.

Cor, what a dump. They can keep it.

But as he was walking away...

BARK

SCREAM

BARK

What's going on in there?

As Arf got out the camera, the door burst open...

...and two big dogs bounded out, dragging Barmy Barney behind them, with the little dog close on his heels.

Arf managed to snap three pictures before he was knocked off his feet by the dogs bounding into him.

A man in a black trilby hat, with a bristly moustache and a spotty cravat, helped Arf back on his feet. He picked up his camera for him.

Here you are, young feller!

Thanks.

That old fool couldn't control those dogs. They're a menace to mothers with children.

sniff sniff

This so-called 'pet sanctuary' ought to be closed down!

Arf thought of Gloria.

Right!

The man handed Arf his card.

Major Nimby.
Chairman of the Residents' Action Group.
3 Potterton Close.

You were a plucky lad though.

Major Nimby slapped Arf on the back.

Well done for snapping those dogs like that. I've only managed to get some shots of the rats infesting this place.

But I saw those dogs. I believe YOU.

So we ought to help one another.

Arf didn't quite understand this.

Why, what do we want to do?

You get your photos developed, as fast as you can — then bring 'em to me at the town hall. I'll be there at half past five.

Arf was puzzled.

What for?

The man looked at Arf more shrewdly.

I'll pay you £25.

26

So Arf went to Mr Sanjay's house. His wife opened the door.

Hello, Arf!

Arf handed over the film.

Then Arf told her all about his story.

I was attacked by two big dogs.

Woof!

And a little dog too!

I took the photos to prove it!

She promised to tell her husband when he came home.

When Arf got back to his own house, there was no one else there. So Arf watched TV and ate three packets of crisps...

...then Mum came back.

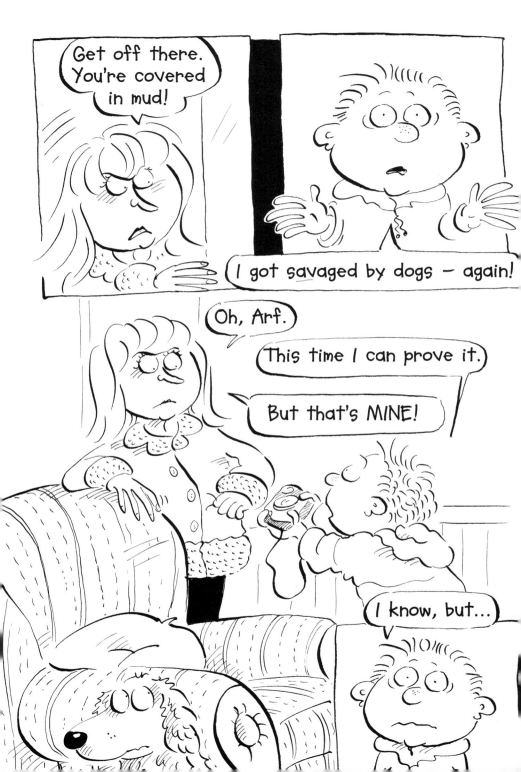

Before Arf could explain himself there was a knock on the door.

33

This was the best bit. Arf opened his mouth. But then through the front room window he caught sight of his sisters coming home from their Saturday jobs.

He waited for them to walk in, then grinned at his elder sister.

I was just going to tell Mr Sanjay about the wild dogs – at your pet place!

There's nothing to smile about, Arf.

Pet place? You mean the sanctuary?

35

Then Arf remembered something. Feeling around in his pocket, he brought out that envelope with Barney's shopping list on the back. He turned it over.

CHAPTER FIVE

Mr Sanjay pressed the doorbell at the old people's home. The warden let them in. He led them along a corridor to room number twelve, Barney Nokes. When Barney opened the door, he looked very sad.

12

Mr Sanjay came straight to the point.

We wondered if you'd very kindly come to our protest meeting, to try to save the pet sanctuary?

Arf rummaged about for his photos only to drop the envelope containing the lottery ticket.

The little dog tried to eat it...

...but Arf snatched it back just in time.

He put it down on the table, next to the local paper, then he showed Barmy Barney the pictures.

The ECHO
PET SANCTUARY
THREATENED

My dogs get cross when I'm cross too.

44

Now Barney looked really angry.

The big dogs looked angry.

The little dog looked even angrier.

You don't know this man, do you, Barney?

I had to work for him once. Nimby's a crooked builder.

The day I quit was the day I found out he was putting live mice through a letter-box, to force an old lady to move out. He wanted to knock her house down and put up a big block of flats.

CHAPTER SIX

It took longer to process Arf's film than Mr Sanjay expected. Then there was lots of traffic.

By the time they got to the town hall the meeting had already started. There were too many people for Arf to see Barney or Bee, or even Gloria, but he could see Major Nimby.

52

Arf found himself being lifted, by Major Nimby's friends, onto the platform beside him.

You've brought me your pictures, I hope?

Arf pulled the photographs out. But they were the ones showing fierce, angry dogs. He put them down on the table, so he could search for the right ones.

But while he was still trying to find them, the major grabbed the first lot and gave them to his assistant.

Arf looked up again at the screen. And yes, there was no doubt about it. The major was emptying a bin bag over the fence.

What's he up to?

Arf got it.

He's feeding his rats!

That's why the place is infested!

Rats?

You cheat!

Nimby's a fraud!

The meeting ended in uproar.

CHAPTER SEVEN

Next Saturday Mum sent Arf to the shop to pick up the local paper.

Back home he opened the front door and was practically knocked off his feet by Barney's two big dogs with their big tongues, trying to lick his face and...

...the little dog too.

WOOF!

Mr Sanjay held up his copy of the local paper, so Arf could read the headline.

Underneath was a detail from one of Arf's photos showing Nimby emptying the bin bag slyly over the fence.

The caption read, 'Dodgy builder exposed!'

Congratulations!

Well done, Arf!